Science
Riddles & Trick Questions
for Kids

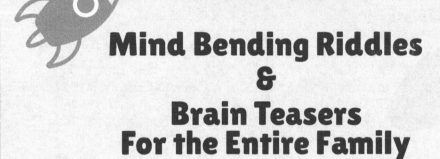

Mind Bending Riddles
&
Brain Teasers
For the Entire Family

With
Fun Illustrations

Riddleland

Table of Contents

	page
Introduction	5
Chapter 1 – Mind-Bending Science Riddles	
Questions	9
Answers	26
Chapter 2 – Try to Work out Who or What Am I?	
Questions	29
Answers	47
Chapter 3 – Bamboozling Brain Teasers	
Questions	51
Answers	71
Chapter 4 – Science of Deduction Logic Puzzles	
Questions	83
Answers	90
Did you enjoy the book?	93
Bonus Book	94
Other books by Riddleland	96
About Riddleland	99
References	100

bonus book

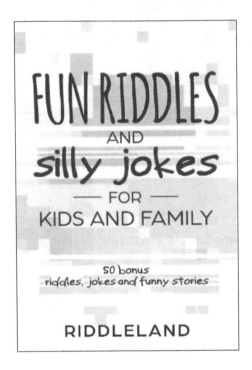

FUN RIDDLES
AND
silly jokes
— FOR —
KIDS AND FAMILY

50 bonus
riddles, jokes and funny stories

RIDDLELAND

SCAN ME

https://pixelfy.me/riddlelandbonus

Thank you for buying this book. We would like to share
a special bonus as a token of appreciation.
It is a collection of 50 original jokes, riddles, and
two funny stories

Introduction

"Science is like magic but real."
~ Unknown

Hello, thank you for picking up a copy this book *Science Riddles for Kids, Mind Bending Riddles & Brain Teasers For the Entire Family*. We hope that your family has as much fun reading it and working out the answers, as we did researching and writing it. Then we used the questions with our children, plus the kids of relatives and friends! As parents ourselves, we're keen to encourage our children and other peoples, to engage with learning science at every opportunity. But we also want to make learning fun, so that it's not a chore!

This science riddle book will cover questions relevant to: Biology, Chemistry and Physics. So, it's a really good all-rounder to help your children with the subject of science at school.

It's not only science skills that will develop by using this book, but by reading aloud, listening, and working out the answers, children's communication, social skills and cognitive skills will also **improve**.

Topics in this book include chemical elements, forces such as gravity, cells, bones, organs, stars, planets, space, the solar system, scientific laws, animals, energy, archaeology, insects, volume, scientific equipment, technology, nature and natural phenomenon.

The 'Who am I?' 'What am I?' section of the book, gets children looking at everyday items connected to science, from a different point of view, and will really test their deductive skills and reasoning. The questions are intriguing and exciting to work out.

The questions in the book, have been well-researched, to be as accurate as possible (though we're always open for discussions and debates). It's a real treasure-trove of science related facts, knowledge and information, where we hope your family will definitely come away learning something new from it. We hope that in many instances, children can use some of the information here in the book as a springboard for further investigation and research, to expand their knowledge as much as possible.

We love spending time as a family, reading, playing games, asking riddles, and learning more about science from this, and we hope that you'll enjoy this too.

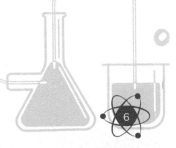

Chapter 1

Mind–Bending Science Riddles

"We should not teach children the sciences
but give them a taste for them."

~ Jean Jacques Rosseau

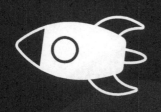

Get ready to go on a
scientific journey filled
with baffling riddles
and puzzling questions.
Can you figure out the
answer to all the riddles
below?

Chapter 1 - Questions

1. What element is based on a famous Marvel character?

_____

2. What element does not like to follow anyone?

_____

3. What is black when you first get it, turns red when you use it, and turns gray when you throw it away?

_____

4. When is it right to say that 100 is also the same as 212?

_____

5. What is a calf but is not part of your body?

Chapter 1 - Questions

6. What is black and white and eats bamboo?

_____

7. What is called Drake but is not the name of a person?

_____

8. What is a lizard but is also a dragon?

_____

9. What's a RAM but it is not part of a computer?

_____

10. What expands when you cool it?

Chapter 1 - Questions

11. What has blades but uses them for flying instead of cutting?

_____

12. What is blue when it is rich, red when it is poor, warm when it is in a bear and cold when it is in a frog?

_____

13. What is something that has a lid, but it is not a mug and has a socket, but it is not a plug?

_____

14. What is something that you use to write, but it is not a pen?

_____

15. What can be good for you and bad for you, can be found inside you and outside you, and does not have a nucleus?

Chapter 1 - Questions

16. What can eat a lot of iron but never get sick?

17. What element can you wear and also use to write?

18. What becomes sharper the more you use it?

Chapter 1 - Questions

19. What comes out at night even though you don't fetch them and gets lost during the day even though they are not stolen?

_____

20. What is something you can look through, but it is not a window and it brings the sky closer to you?

_____

21. What is full of gas but is not a car, has many rings but is not found in a jewelry store, and has a body but is found in space?

_____

22. What is something that seems to float in the sky, but you can never reach it, is shaped like a ball but you can never hold it, and gives off light but you can never turn it off?

_____

23. What slides along its belly, can easily curl up into a ring, has eyes that never close, and has a powerful bite?

Chapter 1 - Questions

24. What is as big as a mountain and yet is part of a belt?

_____

25. What can get full, but it never overflows?

_____

26. What can you catch but you are unable to throw?

_____

27. What is white but is not a sheet of paper and is partly humerus but is not funny?

_____

28. What can run but cannot walk and you always follow it around?

29. What is at the center of gravity?

30. What is found in thermometers and rises when it's hot and also floats in space and is always hot?

Chapter 1 - Questions

31. What is red and floats in space, but appears as an orange dot when you spot it in the sky?

32. What can be sparkling but is not a star, can run but does not have legs, can fall but does not get hurt, and can be used to clean stuff?

33. What has just one big red spot but over 63 moons?

34. What has a slide but is not a playground, has a lens but is not a camera, and is found in a laboratory

35. What spins at a thousand miles an hour but is not a top, has a crust but is not a cookie, and has a molten core?

Chapter 1 - Questions

36. What is as light as a feather but even the strongest person cannot hold it for more than 5 minutes?

37. When do you use He but not to refer to a boy and you use the word periodically?

38. What is found on your body and can be used to measure the distance?

Chapter 1 - Questions

39. What cries without a mouth, flutters without wings, and bites without teeth?

40. What is made of water but fades away when you put it in water?

41. What makes you feel chilly but also shows that you are sick?

Chapter 1 - Questions

42. What is empty but you can still travel in it, has no air but objects still spin in it, and can carry light across long distances?

43. What animal has two eyes in the front and many more behind?

44. What breaks but never falls and you see it the morning?

45. What can you use to point but it is not your finger and it only points to a particular direction, but it is not a map?

46. What is part of breathing if you add 2 and dangerous if you remove 2?

47. What lives when you give it food and dies when you give it water?

48. What is fast, bright, and also comes with a year?

49. What goes up when it is hot, goes down when it is cold and has quite the temper?

Chapter 1 - Questions

50. What makes up everything, but they still float around and are tiny, but you can see them if you use special instruments?

51. What is considered a valuable metal and can also be found in a medal?

52. What can produce ash but is not a bonfire, has a crater but is not on the Moon, and is known to erupt when it has a bad temper?

53. What metallic item do you throw out when you use it, but take it back in when you don't want to use it?

54. What structure has gold within it made by thousands of creatures, but no one guards it and yet its inhabitants walk through the entrance with spear-like weapons, but no one attacks each other?

Chapter 1 - Questions

55. What list has the letter C after B, F after O, and H is the starting letter?

56. What do we have 206 of and they're present in our body?

57. What lives inside a shell when it is young and leaves it when it is older?

58. What is a pearly white chest but has no key or lid and contains a golden treasure inside, but you can't buy anything with it?

Chapter 1 - Questions

59. What is tall when it is young but becomes short when it is old?

60. What helps animals sleep but also gets them through winter?

Chapter 1 - Answers

1. Thorium
2. Lead
3. Coal
4. When you are measuring temperature. 100°C = 212°F
5. A baby cow
6. A panda
7. A male duck
8. Komodo Dragon
9. A male sheep
10. Water
11. Helicopter
12. Blood
13. An eye
14. Your hand
15. Bacteria
16. Rust
17. Carbon, since it is found in diamonds and pencil leads.
18. Your brain
19. Stars
20. A telescope

---

21. Saturn
22. The Sun
23. A snake
24. An asteroid
25. The Moon
26. A cold
27. Bones
28. Your nose
29. The letter "v"
30. Mercury
31. Mars
32. Water
33. Jupiter
34. A microscope
35. Earth
36. Breath
37. When you are referring to Helium
38. Feet
39. The wind
40. An ice cube
41. Cold
42. Space
43. A peacock
44. Dawn
45. A compass
46. Carbon Dioxide (CO2)
47. Fire

---

48. Light
49. Temperature
50. Atoms
51. Gold
52. A volcano
53. An anchor
54. Beehive
55. The periodic table
56. Bones
57. Caterpillar
58. An egg
59. A candle. When it is brand new, it hasn't melted yet. The older it becomes, the more it melts and the shorter it becomes.
60. Hibernation

Chapter 2

Take a guess of Who or What I am ?

"Science is simply the word we use to describe a method of organizing our curiosity."

~ Tim Minchin

These questions make you wonder who or what they are talking about. Can you guess them all?

Chapter 2 - Questions

1. I have one neighbor who has many rings and one who is a dwarf. In total, I have eight neighbors. And strangely, I am the eighth one among them!

What am I?

2. I am used in lamps and in cars. I can start fires and help a vehicle move. I don't react to air, but I don't mix well with water.

What am I?

3. You have two of me I make the world colorful. You cover me when you sleep. You open me when you are awake. You need me to look and you need me to draw.

What am I?

4. You have me with you all the time. If you hold something, you leave me behind. People know I belong to you. You have ten of me.

What am I?

5. I am an organ, but I am not found inside the body. I help you feel but I am not the brain. I protect your bones from the rain and the wind. Yet the rain and the wind can affect me. I come in different colors, yet I am still part of the same. **What am I?**

Chapter 2 - Questions

6. I travel with the clouds and wind. If I fall, I can create streams and help plants grow.

What am I?

7. I use oxygen but I am not the nose. You use me every day and yet, you cannot see me up close. You use me when you talk and when you don't. You use me when you think and when you don't.

What am I?

Chapter 2 - Questions

8. I am found within your bones, but I do not stay there. I move around your body, but I am always carrying something. I can carry oxygen when you need it. And take away carbon dioxide when you don't.

What am I?

9. I study building blocks. I prefer to look at compounds. You can find me in the lab, or I can be used for research. I can help create medicines or I can be a teacher.

Who am I?

10. I examine the past with things I find in the present. I study human behavior but not by looking at humans. I love history, but I also love geography. I love examining tools, but I also love examining caves.

Who am I?

11. I am part of the rose family, but I am not a flower. If you eat me, then I can give your body power. I don't grow on the ground, for you can find me on a tree. Or you might have heard me when talking about gravity.

What am I?

12. Vehicles go over me, but I am not the road. People use me in constructing buildings. Children sometimes play with me, but I am not sand. I can be used in pottery, but I am not clay. I am almost liquid, but I don't flow that easily.

What am I?

Chapter 2 - Questions

13. I build crowns of gold and bridges of silver. I can dig out tiny caves. And I help you smile.

Who am I?

14. I fall down from the sky, but I am not a meteor. I am made of water, but I am not the rain. I survive when it's cold and do not appear when it's hot. If you see me coming down, you might not want to be out.

What am I?

Chapter 2 - Questions

15. I am bigger than a mountain, but you can't see me. I am filled with carbon dioxide and nothing can survive on me. I float in space, but I am not an asteroid. I am your neighbor in space.

What am I?

16. I am quite hot, but I am not the sun. I sometimes leave the clouds, but I am not the rain. I am made of light, but I am not a light bulb. I contain electricity, but I am not a wire.

What am I?

17. I am made of ice, but I am not an ice cube. I float on water, but I am not a type of boat. I can be taller than a mountain, but I am not made of rocks.

What am I?

18. I look at meteors, but I am not a telescope. I can predict the weather, but I am not a satellite. I appear on television, but I am not a TV show. I provide you with weather news, but I am not a newspaper.

Who am I?

19. If you open me and spread me out I can easily fit the size of a tennis court. Yet I am found within your body. I take in one element and I give out another. I deal with gases, either oxygen or the other.

Who am I?

Chapter 2 - Questions

20. I can look at the stars, but I am not a telescope. I know physics but I am not a physics book. I can examine the visible universe, but I am not a satellite.

Who am I?

21. I can grow up to be tall, but I cannot move. I can be chopped but I am not a carrot. I give off carbon dioxide, but I am not a plant. I have many arms, but I am not an animal.

What am I?

Chapter 2 - Questions

22. I am found in food and made into objects. I am quite red, but I am not a fruit. I am in your body and I am also inside a tool. You can find me in doorknobs.

What am I?

23. We are in the ground and in the air. We are in the stars and the birds. Nothing can exist without us. Everything in the universe is filled with us.

What am I?

24. I am found within walls and lying around. I was used in both prehistoric and modern times. I rhyme with the word bone.

What am I?

25. I can grow plants and vegetables. But I am not a tree. I am a kind of activity. You can use me for growing corn and wheat. I produce things that you can eat

What am I?

26. I can travel up to a hundred miles an hour. I usually exit through the nose when someone tickles it.

What am I?

Chapter 2 - Questions

27. You breathe me out and plants breathe me in. For some, I am dangerous, but for others, I turn into food. I have a "sea" and "oh" in my name.

What am I?

28. I contain oxygen and I am part of the stratosphere. I am not a plane. I protect you from the sun's harmful rays. But the sun makes me. Without me, the Earth would be hot.

What am I?

29. I have the colors blue, yellow and green. I also have violet, red, orange, and indigo. I am seen in the sky, but I am not a cloud.

What am I?

30. I go round and round, but I am not the merry-go-round. I was invented in 3,500 BC, but I am not a ball. I help things move, but I am not a vehicle. You can find me on cars and airplanes, but not on boats.

What am I?

31. You can see through me, but I am not air. You can hold me in your hands, but I am not water. I help make and build things, but I am not plastic. I can be a part of other things, but I cannot float in the air.

What am I?

Chapter 2 - Questions

32. I am a fruit and a bean. If I am ground, then I become a powder. But if I am mixed, then I become a drink. Sometimes I can be quite acidic. I am born in Africa and Brazil at the same time.

What am I?

33. I start with an S and end with an L. I am in kitchen objects and inside a bell. You find me in keys, nuts, bolts, and spoons. I am there in vehicles and a metal stool. I am a metal.

What am I?

Chapter 2 - Questions

34. I am an important metal. I can be found in airplanes and screws. Sometimes, I am not a hard-inflexible metal. Since I am found in foil that covers your food and vegetables!

What am I?

35. I am an earful. But I am not part of your body. I grow from the ground from a small seed. You can find me in cereals, peanut butter, and syrup.

What am I?

36. I am flexible, but I am not plastic. I am found in tires, but I am not found in the rims. I am found on one end of a pencil, but not in the other. I am found in bands, but not the ones that play in concerts.

What am I?

37. I pump liquid, but I do not pump water. I beat constantly, but I am not a drum. You need me to live, but I am not an object you consciously use. I live within you, but I am not a bone.

What am I?

38. I am something people are scared of, but I am not heights. Some of my family members can bite, but I am not a snake. I have eight legs and I have a web.

What am I?

Chapter 2 - Questions

39. If I am heated, I expand. If I am cooled, I contract. You can find me in your body. And you can find me out at sea. I may not be "airy." But if you would like to, then I can definitely be.

Who am I?

40. I am a vibration, but it is not sound that causes me. I can topple buildings, but I am not a bulldozer. You can measure me on a scale. I can cause a lot of disturbance.

What am I?

Chapter 2 - Questions

41. I add flavor in pizzas and pastas. I am usually as white as snow. But I am not a type of cheese. I am a collection of tiny crystals. I can be used on meat or vegetables.

What am I?

42. I come in sheets, but I am not a metal. I am usually white, but you can find me in different colors. I can hold a painting, but I am not an easel. I am a surface for ink and print, but I am not a printer.

What am I?

Chapter 2 - Questions

43. I am a liquid, but I am not water. I am quite sticky, but I am not glue. I am sweet, but I am not chocolate. I can be found inside a comb, but I am not on your hair. I am made by an insect, but I am not a web.

What am I?

44. There are billions of us floating around. I'm not in the sea or the ground. If you see me from afar, I am tiny. But if you see me up close, I am gigantic. You live within one of us. The whole universe is filled with us.

What are we?

Chapter 2 - Questions

45. I cause things to rise, but I am not an elevator. You can feel me on your skin, but I am not the wind. Fire causes me, but I am not the flame. I can affect the thermometer, but I am not the cold.

What am I?

46. I live in a tall home, but it's not a building. I can live in the desert, but I am not a camel. I create mounds and I am like an ant.

What am I?

47. You can find me in the mountains and the creek. I have no mouth and I can speak every language. I have no brain, but I answer every cry. I usually have the last word.

What am I?

48. When you look at me, I look back at you. When you raise your left hand, I raise my right. I am your twin, yet I am not with you. I am found on surfaces, yet you cannot hold me.

What am I?

49. I provide cover, but I am not a lid. I have many strands, but I am not a cloth. I am always with you, but I am not an object. I come in different colors, but I am not a pair of shoes.

What am I?

Chapter 2 - Questions

50. I am white, but I am not the snow. You add me to coffee, but I am not milk. You can find me in fruits, and in sweet foods.

What am I?

51. I have scales but you can't use me to measure weight. I feed on nectar, but I am not the honeybee. I have wings, but I am not a moth. I am colorful, but I am not a bird.

What am I?

Chapter 2 - Questions

52. I am bouncy but I am not a trampoline. I live in lakes, but I am not a fish. I can be colorful and live on land.

What am I?

53. Separately, I am red, blue, and yellow. Together, I am black.

What am I?

54. Worms create me and you wear me. I am used to make many clothes.

What am I?

55. I am a wave, but I am not found at sea. I am a vibration caused when things move. You can sense me, but not through your skin. You use a tissue that is found within.

What am I?

56. I can run but I don't walk. I have a mouth, but I never talk. I have a head, but I never weep. I have a bed, but I do not sleep.

What am I?

Chapter 2 - Questions

57. I wear armor, but I am not a knight. I wear it day and night. I walk on all fours and I can swim in the sea.

What am I?

58. I am cold, but I am not the temperature. I am solid, but I am not an ice cube. You can find me in the South Pole, and I have a large land mass.

What am I?

Chapter 2 - Questions

59. I am inside an atom, but I am not a proton. I am negatively charged.

What am I?

60. I examine plants, but I am not an animal. In fact, I study all about them.

Who am I?

H_2O

Chapter 2 - Answers

1. Neptune
2. Oil
3. Eyes
4. Fingerprints
5. Your skin.
6. Rain
7. The human brain
8. Red blood cells

9. A chemist
10. An archeaologist
11. An apple
12. Mud
13. A dentist
14. Hail
15. Venus
16. Lightning

17. An iceberg
18. A meteorologist
19. Lungs
20. An astronomer
21. A tree
22. Copper
23. Matter
24. Stone

---

25. Farming
26. A sneeze
27. Carbon Dioxide
28. Ozone
29. Rainbow
30. A wheel
31. Glass
32. Coffee. Coffee bean is also an acceptable answer.

33. Steel
34. Aluminum
35. Corn
36. Rubber
37. The heart
38. A spider
39. Water
40. An earthquake
41. Salt

42. Paper
43. Honey
44. Galaxies
45. Heat
46. Termite
47. An echo
48. A reflection
49. Hair

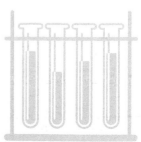

50. Sugar

51. Butterfly

52. Frog

53. Primary colors. Even "colors" is an acceptable answer.

54. Silk

55. Sound

56. The river

57. A turtle

58. Antarctica

59. Electron

60. Botanist

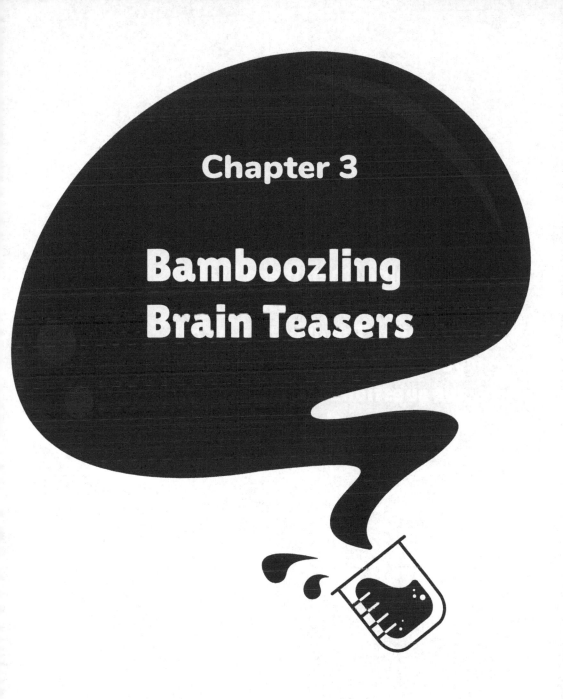

Chapter 3

Bamboozling Brain Teasers

"Science is more than a body of knowledge
It's a way of thinking, a way of skeptically
interrogating the universe."

~ Carl Sagan

When you want to challenge your mind, then these brain teasers are sure to keep you guessing. The question is, can you get to the solution before the questions stump you? Let's find out!

Chapter 3 - Questions

1. What walks on four feet in the morning, and then walks on two feet in the afternoon, and then walks on three feet in the evening?

_____

2. Before hydrogen was discovered, what was the first element in the periodic table?

_____

3. Peter said to Adam, "Did you know that I once went to the zoo and saw a kangaroo walking backwards?" Adam looked at Peter and said, "Did that really happen? I can't believe that's true!" Do you think what Peter said is right?

_____

4. Now imagine that you are balancing a broom horizontally on your finger. Your finger is on the broom's center of gravity. The broom is balanced perfectly, and it does not fall. You mark the center of gravity on the broom and using that mark, you cut the broom into two pieces. You have a short piece and a long piece. Which of the following statements is true?
a. The short piece is heavier.
b. The long piece is heavier.
c. Both the pieces will weigh the same.
d. Your mother might find both pieces and scold you!

Chapter 3 - Questions

5. You have entered a cabin and it is pitch black. You want to create light, but you have just one match with you. However, you also have a few other objects near you. These are a newspaper, a lamp, a candle, or a fire. Which object do you light first?

6. One day, a boy noticed a man blowing balloons using a pipe. These balloons would then float up into the sky. Excited, the boy got some balloons for himself and took them home. He blew into the balloons and when they were filled, he let them go. But they did not float up. Why?

Chapter 3 - Questions

7. One day, the blue whale said to his friends, "I am the largest living organism in the world." But his friend, the shark, did not believe him. Why is that?

8. Jack is on the top of a mountain and it is snowing all around him. He is freezing and he has no tent to use. However, Jack used a single sock and now he is not only feeling warm, but he has a place to sleep. What did Jack do?

9. Sarah and her friends decided to play a prank on a group of astronomers who were having a meeting that night. They called up the astronomers and told them, "I am an astronomer and I just saw a meteorite fly through the sky." The astronomers hung up the phone because they knew Sarah was not telling the truth. How did they figure it out?

10. There were three friends who were trying to show off their special talents: The first friend said, "I can cartwheel three times in a row." The second friend said, "I can do a backflip while holding my nose." The third friend said, "I can lick my elbows." Which one of the friends is not telling the truth?

Chapter 3 - Questions

11. What came first, the egg or the chicken?

12. Peter and his best friend William went fishing one day when they saw a shark slowly circling the boat. William suggested using the oars to row as quickly to the shore as possible. Peter suggested another idea by saying, "Don't worry. Stay calm and wait it out. Once the sharks fall asleep, we can easily row the boat away and reach the safety of the shore." Was William right or was Peter right?

Chapter 3 - Questions

13. There were three best friends, and two of them were twins. The twins used to live separately while the third friend used to live on his own. One day, the three friends decided to meet each other. But as soon as they met, they turned into a liquid! What just happened?

14. A scientist had once approached a man. He told the man that he had a flask that contained a liquid that was capable of dissolving anything it touched. The scientist told the man that the liquid was very expensive. However, the man did not believe the scientist's claims. Why?

15. It is said that the Earth weighs around 6 sextillion tons (that's one thousand million million million tons!) Now imagine that you took one sextillion tons of stone and added it to the Earth. How much would the Earth weigh?

16. A bird was able to fly faster than a plane. But the plane hadn't slowed down one bit. How was it possible?

17. One student said to his friend, "Can you name one animal that has the YY chromosome?" The friend replied by saying, "I don't think I can answer that question." Why did the friend say that?

Chapter 3 - Questions

18. A young girl had ice at home. She wanted to melt the ice and turn it into water. But when she put the ice in a microwave to heat it, she saw something surprising. The ice turned to gas immediately! Why did that happen?

19. The biology teacher said to his students, "Kids, today we are going to learn about the cranium." One of the kids said, "Don't you mean skull?" The teacher replied, "That's what I said." What did he mean?

Chapter 3 - Questions

20. One student said to his friend, "Isn't it fascinating that the sun is responsible for day and night?" His friend said, "Well, that is not actually true." Why did his friend say that?

---

21. When you combine the words below, they spell out one single word. What word is that?

Hydrogen, Oxygen, Phosphorus

---

22. The teacher said to the kids, "Hello everyone! Today, we are going to study Newton's Second Law of Motion where every action has an equal and opposite reaction." One of the kids said, "But we cannot study that!" Why did the kid say that?

---

23. One day, Susan decided to ask John a question. She told him that there is something that rises in Hawaii, can flow in San Francisco, but stands still in Antarctica. John immediately told her what it was. What was John's answer?

---

24. Adam and his family were out in the backyard. There was no light in the backyard, except for the moonlight. Yet they still received the sunlight as well. How is that possible?

Chapter 3 - Questions

25. Adam was about to brush his teeth when he looked at his older brother and said, "Today, I am going to clean all 34 teeth properly." His older brother said, "I am afraid you cannot do that." Why did the older brother say that?

26. Amy saw her friend Sue training ducks to move in a particular direction. When Sue held up a blue card, the ducks would move to the right and when she held up a red card, the ducks would move to the left. Amy decided that she would try the same with her dogs. But her dogs didn't respond to the blue or red card the way the ducks did. Why was that?

Chapter 3 - Questions

27. It is a cold night and you want to cover yourself in something warm. You have two options. Which of the following would you use?
a. A single two-inch thick blanket.
b. Two blankets that are each one-inch thick.

28. You have a cup of water with just one ice cube in it. The ice cube melts. Which one of the following statements is true?
a. There is more water in the cup.
b. The water level remains the same.
c. There is less water in the cup.

29. A scientist was talking to his scientist friend and boasting about his recent discovery. The scientist said, "I sent a probe to Venus and we just found out that that summers in Venus can be very hot." The scientist's friend looked up at him and said, "You are wrong." Why was the scientist wrong?

30. Brian asked Matthew, "How can I get taller? Matthew said, "Just go to space." Why did Matthew say that?

31. A NASA scientist suggested that astronauts can collect dust from the moon by simply using a vacuum cleaner to suck up the dust. However, another scientist told him the idea would not work. Why is that?

Chapter 3 - Questions

32. Mary was preparing the vegetable salad. She said, "I will need the following vegetables: cucumber, potato, tomato, and carrot." Sue looked at her friend and said, "Then your salad won't be a vegetable salad anymore." Why did Sue say that?

33. You have with you a bucket filled with one gallon of cold water. You have another bucket with you that is filled with one gallon of hot water. Which of the following statements is true?

a. The hot water is heavier.

b. The cold water is heavier.

c. Both the hot and the cold water weigh the same.

Chapter 3 - Questions

34. Amber looked at her friend Terry and said, "Elephants have almost no predators. Yet they have such big ears. Why do they have such big ears if they don't use them to listen? They must be pretty useless." Terry said, "Actually, that's where you are wrong." Why did Terry think the ears were important to the elephants?

35. Brian was playing with the tennis ball when suddenly, it disappeared down a hole. The hole was fairly deep, and Brain could not reach down and get the ball. The hole also had a curve in the middle, which meant that Brian could not use a stick to get the ball out. In the end, Brian managed to get the ball out and continue playing with it. What did Brian do?

36. Ryan and David were riding their bikes home when they came upon a lake. Ryan said to David, "I bet I can make a rock float on water." David said, "No you can't! No rock floats on water. I'll give you $10 if you can make it happen." Ryan won the $10. Why did he win?

Chapter 3 - Questions

37. Robert and Peter decided to write a message in invisible ink. Robert had an idea. He went to where his mother kept the fruits and vegetables and picked up an item. What item did he pick?

38. A scientist was looking into a glass that contained a liquid. He looked at his assistant and said, "This glass contains a liquid that is at minus 40 degrees." His assistant looked at him and said, "Would that be minus 40 degrees Celsius or minus 40 degrees Fahrenheit?" The scientist looked at his assistant and said, "It does not matter." Why did the scientist say that?

Chapter 3 - Questions

39. James and Charles were riding home when they had to go down a slope. The saw a nearby tree catching fire. James said that they should go up the slope because it would take time for the fire to catch up to them. Charles said that they should be going down instead since the fire would take longer to catch up with them. Who was right?

40. You have launched two probes. One has landed on Venus and one fell back to Earth. The one that landed on Venus is named "Probe 1" while the one that fell back on Earth is "Probe 2." After a year, Probe 2 has turned one year old since it was created. However, Probe 1 is still not a year old. Why is that?

41. A bird was heading towards a power line. He decided to sit on top of it. However, his friend shouted a warning. "No don't! You are going to get electrocuted!" But the bird did not listen to his friend. Why?

Chapter 3 - Questions

42. Imagine that a bird is carrying a small oxygen tank and is now flying on the moon. Now that there is a small tank on the bird's back, would the bird fly faster, slower, or at the same speed that it could fly on Earth?

43. An archaeologist asked his colleague, "When I find the fossil bones, do I put them in plastic bags or carry them by hand?" The colleague said, "The first thing to remember is that you would never be able to touch a fossil bone." Why did the colleague say that?

Chapter 3 - Questions

44. A scientist said to his friend, "I am going to create a device that can withstand the heat of the sun. I will then be able to take the carbon dioxide produced by the sun and then convert it into oxygen." The friend replied, "There is just one itsy-bitsy problem." What was the problem?

45. Your friend is pushing a large box. You walk over to him and ask him what he is doing. He says, "Well, I am applying a little acceleration to this box, so it moves faster." You look at him and tell him that it does not work. Why is that?

46. John wanted to build his muscles. In order to do so, he asked his friend Ray for help. Ray said that John should try eating more iron, since that will develop his muscles even more. John did not believe that Ray's suggestion would help him. Why is that?

47. I would like to change the color of a leaf. What I do is take a leaf, dip it in rose-colored water, and then shine a light on it. Do you think this will change the color of the leaf?

48. Two frogs fell into a jar of liquid. The jar was pretty tall, so the frogs couldn't easily get out. After a few minutes, one frog swam around in circles until eventually, the liquid became hard and the frog could jump out. The other frog was surprised and asked his friend how he did it. What was the solution?

Chapter 3 - Questions

49. Adam said to his friend Jacob that he bets $10 that he will be able to fold a square piece of paper ten times. Jacob looked at him and said, "No you cannot. You will lose." Why did Jacob say that?

50. A man was driving a truck when he came across a long bridge. The sign near the bridge said that nothing over 4 tons can cross the bridge. Thankfully, the truck weighed exactly 4 tons. About halfway over the bridge, a little bird lands on top of the truck, increasing its weight slightly. The man began to panic. However, his friend, who was sitting in the passenger seat, told the man that nothing will happen. He said that since the truck used something, it became lighter. What did the truck use?

Chapter 3 - Questions

51. A physics student wanted to learn more about the Three Laws of Motion. He went over to the physics section and began to read the discoveries of Albert Einstein. A few minutes later, the student's friend recommended a better way to learn about the Three Laws of Motion. What was that way?

52. A patient came to the doctor with a bad cough. The doctor took one look at the patient and then turned to his assistant. He said, "I would like you to give this patient some fungal waste to drink." The assistant was shocked and said, "Surely doctor! That is not what you mean?" Yet the doctor was actually right. Why?

53. One astronaut said to another, "When we are in space, I will shout out your name so you can hear me." The second astronaut said, "But I won't respond to you." Why did the second astronaut say that?

54. The student asked his teacher, "How can I see ultraviolet light?" The teacher said, "If you can become small and start making webs." Why did the teacher say that?

55. Two brothers wanted to call their dog home. The younger brother decided that he would place a bowl of dog food at the entrance of the house while the older brother said that he would try calling the dog's name. After an hour, the dog returned. But which brother's idea had worked?

Chapter 3 - Questions

56. A blacksmith has a hot piece of steel. He now has to cool it down quickly. He has with him a bucket of water and a bucket of oil. The blacksmith's apprentice tells him that he should quickly drop the piece of steel into the water to cool it down. But the blacksmith tells the apprentice that it would be a bad idea to do that. Why did the blacksmith say this?

water   oil

57. A scientist looked into his microscope for a while. He looked up from the microscope and turned to his lab assistant. He told him, "I am looking at multiplication and division happen at the same time." The lab assistant was confused. "That is not possible sir. Such a thing cannot happen at the same time." But the scientist was right. Why is that?

Chapter 3 - Questions

58. Adam tried to sneak up on a rabbit. He made no sound and the rabbit could not smell him. The rabbit was looking away from Adam, but it still found out he was there and ran away. How did the rabbit find out?

59. Marie was drinking hot chocolate when she said, "It's so wonderful that so many seeds are used to make this chocolate." Her friend Emma said, "That's not wonderful at all." Why did Emma say that?

Chapter 3 - Questions

60. The bee looked at the butterfly and said, "I bet if you had no mouth, you wouldn't be able to taste this delicious honey." The butterfly said, "I still can, actually." Why did the butterfly say that?

Chapter 3 - Answers

1. A human being in various stages of life. As a baby, the human being crawls on four legs. As an adult, the human being walks on two legs and when the human is old, he might use a walking cane to aid him.

2. It was still the hydrogen. It just wasn't discovered yet!

3. What Peter said is not true at all. Kangaroos cannot move backwards, unlike many other animals of the animal kingdom.

4. The shorter piece is heavier. Why? Because the shorter piece also includes the brush and the brush cap. And why does the broom balance? It is because the "center" of gravity is not always at the "center" of the broom. It is at the part where you are able to balance it properly.

5. You light the match first. Only then can you light anything else in the room.

6. The man was using a pipe, which is usually connected to a cylinder that contains helium. Since helium is lighter than air, it causes the balloon to float. Carbon dioxide, on the other hand, is not lighter than air and therefore, the balloon gently falls to the ground.

7. The blue whale is the largest mammal in the world. But the largest organism is a fungus. It grows in Oregon and covers nearly 2,200 acres of land!

8. Jack dug a hole in the snow in the shape of a sock. He is sleeping inside this hole, which is protecting him from the cold and is giving him a place to sleep.

Chapter 3 - Answers

9. When a meteor is still in the air, it is called a meteor. But it is only called a meteorite when it lands on the Earth.

Bonus fact : The object itself is called a meteoroid when it is in space! It does not become a meteor unless it enters the Earth's atmosphere and does not become a meteorite unless it hits the ground.

10. The third friend was not telling the truth. You see, no matter how hard we try, our bodies are not flexible enough to allow us to lick the elbows.

11. The egg, since the dinosaurs laid eggs long before chickens even came into existence!

12. William was right. Why was Peter wrong? It is because sharks don't sleep!

Bonus fact : So how do sharks sleep? They don't. Shark brains have two states: active and resting. When the brain is active, sharks are moving about and looking for food. When the brain is resting, sharks are still moving! Yes indeed! However, they are not aware of their surroundings.

Chapter 3 - Answers

13. The three friends were hydrogen and oxygen. The twins were the two elements of hydrogen. When they got together, they became H2O, which is the molecular formula for water.

14. The liquid hadn't dissolved the flask yet!

15. The Earth would still weigh 6 sextillion tons. That is because all the stone that you would use comes from the Earth itself.

16. The bird was inside the plane and it flew from the back of the plane to the front.

17. The reason the friend could not answer the question is because there is no YY chromosome! The human DNA has XY and XX chromosomes.

18. The girl was heating dry ice. Dry ice is nothing but carbon dioxide. This is why, when you heat it, it does not turn into a liquid, but transforms directly into gas. This process, where a solid directly turns into gas, is called "sublimation."

19. The scientific name for a skull is "cranium." When the professor mentioned cranium, he was referring to the skull.

20. It is because the earth is constantly spinning that the line between day and night is always moving around the planet.

21. They spell the word HOP. Hydrogen is represented by H on the periodic table. Oxygen is represented by O on the periodic table. Phosphorus is represented by P on the periodic table.

Chapter 3 - Answers

22. The reason the kids could not study was because it was not Newton's second law the teacher mentioned. It was Newton's third law!

23. It was water. The reason is that Hawaii is really hot and therefore, water can evaporate easily and rise. San Francisco has moderate temperatures and therefore, water stays in liquid form. However, the temperatures in Antarctica are extremely cold. Water turns to ice easily when in Antarctica and stays still.

24. The moon reflects the light of the sun. Basically, what you call moonlight is simply the sunlight reflected at you!

25. Adam could not brush all 34 of his teeth because he does not have 34 teeth. The adult human body only has about 32 teeth!

26. The dogs were colorblind. However, the ducks were not, since ducks are known to recognize colors better than humans can!

27. The answer is b: "Two blankets that are each one-inch thick".

Bonus fact : When you place two blankets that are each one-inch thick, then you have a layer of air between those blankets. That air also acts as a protective layer, helping you stay warmer!

Chapter 3 - Answers

28. The answer is b: "The water level remains the same". When you add ice into water, you raise the level of the water a little bit. Remember that ice is still water. When the ice melts, it turns into water and that's why it does not affect the water level around it.

29. Venus does not have any seasons.

Bonus fact : In order for a planet to have seasons, it needs to tilt on its axis slightly. This way, one pole faces the sun while the other faces away from the sun. Venus, on the other hand, does not tilt on its axis.

30. Gravity does not pull you down in space. Hence, you can become taller.

31. There is no air on the moon and the vacuum cleaner won't be able to suck in the dust.

32. Tomatoes are not vegetables. They are fruit! That is why the salad won't be called a vegetable salad anymore.

33. The answer is b: "The cold water is heavier". Cold water is heavier than hot water, albeit slightly, because the molecules in cold water are denser. This means that the molecules are packed tightly together.

Chapter 3 - Answers

34. Elephants use their long ears to keep themselves warm. It's like a layer of blanket!

35. Brian filled the hole up with water. The ball floated to the surface.

36. He used a rock called pumice!

Bonus fact : Pumice is a rock that is created when volcanoes erupt. They contain many gas bubbles inside them. When you toss them on water, they begin to float.

37. Robert picked a lemon.

Bonus fact : In You can use lemon to create invisible ink. All you have to do is squeeze the juice of the lemon into a glass and write something using the liquid. When you bring the paper close to a source of heat, then the letters appear in a reddish-brown color. But do not try this at home and do not attempt to play with fire!

Chapter 3 - Answers

38. Because minus 40 degrees Celsius is the same as minus 40 degrees Fahrenheit.

39. Charles was right. Hot air rises and causes the flames to rise upward faster.

40. A year on Earth is just one day on Venus. Even though Probe 2 spent one year on Earth, Probe 1 only saw a single day complete itself. Venus goes around the sun much more slowly than the Earth. That is why, by the time a single day is over on Venus, Earth is ready to pass it by for a second year.

41. Birds do not get electrocuted if they sit on a power line.

Bonus fact : Electricity flows in a loop. When a bird sits on a wire, then the electricity cannot flow through it. However, if the bird was sitting on two lines at the same time, then the electricity can flow through one line, through the bird, and then flow to the other line.

42. What did we learn earlier? The Moon has no atmosphere. Therefore, the bird won't be able to fly at all.

43. Fossils are not the remains of living things. They cannot be the bones or other material of those living things. Fossils are the rocks that hold the remains.

Chapter 3 - Answers

44. The sun does not produce too much carbon dioxide, even though it is so hot. 98% of the sun is made up of hydrogen and helium.

45. You don't apply acceleration to push something. You apply force.

46. Iron does not help the muscles grow strong. You need proteins for muscle-building. Which is why you shouldn't forget to have your greens! Greens like spinach are a good source of iron.

47. It wouldn't change the color of the leaf. Leaves are green because of the presence of chlorophyll in them. The chlorophyll reflects green light back at you.

48. The liquid was cream. When you mix cream, then it turns into butter. One frog was able to thicken the cream and leap out just in time.

49. You cannot fold a piece of paper more than seven times

50. The truck used gas. Since the gas in the truck's fuel tank was converted to exhaust, the weight of the truck was reduced. The bird could sit on the truck and enjoy a free ride!

51. The friend suggested reading about the discoveries of Isaac Newton, since it was Newton who had first discovered the Three Laws of Motion.

52. Fungal waste is actually used in manufacturing alcohol. Some form of alcohol is then used in cough syrup. Don't worry, it is not harmful and in fact, doctors even use a form of alcohol to clean your wounds!

53. Sound does not travel in space since there is no air. Space is filled with vacuum.

Chapter 3 - Answers

54. The teacher was referring to a spider. Spiders are capable of seeing ultraviolet (or UV) lights.

55. The younger brother's idea had worked. Dogs have a stronger sense of smell than hearing. They are able to track objects and people for miles.

56. If you drop the steel into the water, then the water will start boiling. This would cause the blacksmith to hurt his hands. If he puts it into the oil, then it will cool the metal more quickly.

Bonus fact : At this point, you might be wondering why the oil did not catch fire. Here is an interesting fact for you to know. Did you know that if you throw a burning matchstick on gasoline it does not cause it to catch fire? This is because the burning point of gasoline is actually very high.

Chapter 3 - Answers

57. The scientist was looking at cell division. Whenever your cells split up, they divide. However, when they split up, more of them are produced, which happens because they multiply. This is why cells are capable of dividing and multiplying at the same time.

58. Rabbits can see behind them without turning their heads.

59. Because chocolate is not made using seeds. Chocolate comes from beans that grow on trees.

60. Butterflies taste using their feet.

Chapter 4

The Science of Deduction Logic Puzzles

"A scientist is not a person who gives the right answers. He is the one who asks the right questions."

~ Unknown

These puzzles defy logic.
Or do they? If you read them
carefully, you might just find
the clue you have been looking
for. How many of the puzzles
can you solve?

$E=MC^2$

Chapter 4 - Questions

1. There is a one-story house that is completely made from metal. The walls are metallic. The furniture is made from metal. The doors are completely made from metal. Even all the couches and beds in the house are metallic. What are the stairs made of?

2. What letters are found in every element of the periodic table?

3. John says that he can throw the ball up in the air in such a manner that it will change direction and still end up returning to him. Is that even possible?

4. A girl fell off a 20-foot ladder and yet, she was unhurt. How is that possible?

5. Grandpa stepped out of the house for a walk. Suddenly, it started raining heavily. He didn't bring a hat or an umbrella with him and pretty soon, he was soaked. But despite the fact that his clothes and shoes were soaked, his hair was not wet. How is that possible?

Chapter 4 - Questions

6. John looks at Adam and said that he would like to find a mammal with scales. Adam says that he might find that rather difficult indeed. Why did Adam say that?

7. A man said to his friend, "I think I am injured. Could you get me a kit so that I can treat my wounds?" The man's friend brought back a kit, but suddenly, the kit leaped from his hands and escaped! What just happened?

8. The leopard decided to get his family members together. However, when the family arrived at the leopard's home, they were surprised to find a lion sitting there! Why was the lion present?

9. A doctor was about to prescribe antibiotics to a patient who had the common cold. His colleague told him not to do that. Why did the colleague stop the doctor?

10. Lucas said, "I bet I can throw something down a hole and no matter what you do, you will never be able to get it back." Lucas could do something like that. How?

Chapter 4 - Questions

11. Amy decided to boil water quickly to make some tea. She decided to raise the temperature so that water boiled at 100°C. But when she decided to make the tea, she realized that she could no longer do it. Why is that?

12. A man said to his friend, "From tomorrow onwards, I am going to be an early riser. I am going to wake up the very second that my region of the Earth faces the sun." The man's friend looked at him and said, "You might have to be faster than that." What did the man's friend mean by that?

Chapter 4 - Questions

13. A doctor said to his colleague, "I am going to study a single piece of coiled gene from a DNA tonight. Would you like to join me?" The colleague replied, "I wish I could. But aren't you forgetting something?" What was the doctor forgetting?

14. A young boy was looking at how light touches a prism and then changes into different colors. He looked at his friend and said, "I like how the prism reflects the light." The boy's friend said, "Thankfully, it is not doing that." What was the prism doing?

15. If you were talking about a sweet potato, then what would you be talking about?
a. leaf
b. stem
c. branch

16. James said to Victor, "I am ready to run. I have a lot of kinetic energy stored up, since that is going to help me with motion." Victor said, "That is true. Kinetic energy is what is going to help you move. However, you might need more than just kinetic energy to run." Why did Victor say that?

17. All you have to do is move one single plate and you can cause an earthquake. That statement is actually true. But why is that?

Chapter 4 - Questions

18. Peter said that he would be bringing his friend Joey to the party. When Joey arrived, everyone was surprised to see him with a tail. What happened to Joey?

19. Rebecca said, "All I need is helium since that is the lightest element in existence." She is not exactly right. Why is that?

Chapter 4 - Questions

20. Jerome had homework about plants, animals, fungi, yeast, and bacteria. He walked to his friend Dylan and said that he would be studying plants, animals, fungi, and bacteria during the weekend. His friend Dylan asked, "What about yeast?" Jerome replied, "I already mentioned it." How had Jerome mentioned yeast without actually having mentioned the word?

21. Sally once said, "The 'N' on my magnet is pointing towards the north. But I don't think it is actually pointing to the north." She is absolutely right! Why is that?

22. Matthew said, "I just need light and I will be able to make you listen to the radio with it." That could be possible. Why is that?

Chapter 4 - Answers

1. It is a one-story house. There are no stairs.

2. The letters e-l-e-m-e-n-t.

3. Yes, it is. He just has to throw the ball straight up in the air. Gravity stops the ball and pulls it back down, which is a change in direction. It will then fall back down straight towards John.

4. She fell off the lowest rung of the 20-foot ladder and therefore, she was unhurt.

5. Grandpa was bald.

6. Only reptiles have scales. No mammal in the world has any scales.

7. The man's friend accidentally brought a baby rabbit. Young rabbits are called kits.

8. Because the lion is closely related to the leopard.

9. Antibiotics are used to fight bacterial infections.They have no effect on viruses. The common cold is caused by a type of virus.

10. He was talking about a black hole. If anything enters the black hole, it does not get out. Even light is completely absorbed by the black hole.

Bonus fact : Did you know that black holes were once stars that were living? These stars are like our sun and when they run out of fuel, they sometimes turn into a black hole. But our sun won't turn into a black hole. It is not big enough to do that!

Chapter 4 - Answers

11. 100°C is water's boiling point. When water reaches that temperature, then it turns into gaseous form quickly.

Bonus fact : Every time you are looking at the sun, you are looking into the past. Since it takes 8 minutes for the light from the sun to reach us, we are looking at the sun as it was eight minutes ago! This means that the sun is actually in a different location. Now that is one way to time travel!

12. It takes 8 minutes for the sun's rays to reach the Earth. So, the man won't be able to wake up at the same second that the Earth faces the sun.

13. A single piece of coiled DNA is called a chromosome. A good doctor should be able to remember that basic fact.

14. It was refracting the light.

15. None of the options would describe a sweet potato. Sweet potatoes are an example of a modified root.

16. You need kinetic energy to move, but you need potential energy to start moving.

Chapter 4 - Answers

17. Earthquakes are caused because of the movement of tectonic plates. All it takes is one single tectonic plate moving and the ground starts shaking!

18. Nothing happened. Peter brought a young Kangaroo. Young kangaroos are called joeys.

19. That is not true. Hydrogen is the lightest element in existence.

20. Yeast is a type of fungi.

21. When it comes to magnets, opposite poles attract. The direction that 'N' points towards is not the North, but the South! In fact, the only reason why we call the North as the North and the South as the South is because when reading a map, north points up and south points down. Wait a minute, in that case, are we actually living in the opposite hemisphere? I wonder.

22. It is possible because radio waves are a kind of light.

Bonus fact : Radio waves, microwaves, infrared, and gamma rays are all different types of light.

Did you enjoy the book?

If you did, we are ecstatic. If not, please write your complaint to us and we will ensure we fix it.

If you're feeling generous, there is something important that you can help me with – tell other people that you enjoyed the book.

Ask a grown-up to write about it on Amazon. When they do, more people will find out about the book. It also lets Amazon know that we are making kids around the world laugh. Even a few words and ratings would go a long way.

If you have any ideas or jokes that you think are super funny, please let us know. We would love to hear from you. Our email address is -

riddleland@riddlelandforkids.com

bonus book

FUN RIDDLES
AND
silly jokes
— FOR —
KIDS AND FAMILY

50 bonus
riddles, jokes and funny stories

RIDDLELAND

SCAN ME

https://pixelfy.me/riddlelandbonus

Thank you for buying this book. We would like to share
a special bonus as a token of appreciation.
It is a collection of 50 original jokes, riddles, and
two funny stories

CONTEST

Would you like your jokes and riddles to be featured in our next book?

We are having a contest to see who are the smartest or funniest boys and girls in the world!

1) Creative and Challenging Riddles
2)Tickle Your Funny Bone Contest

Parents, please email us your child's "Original" Riddle or Joke, **and he or she could win a $25 Amazon gift card and be featured in our next book.**

Here are the rules:

1) It must be challenging for the riddles and funny for the jokes!

2) It must be 100% original and not something from the Internet! It is easy to find out!

3) You can submit both a joke and a riddle as they are two separate contests.

4) No help from the parents unless they are as funny as you.

5) Winners will be announced via email or our Facebook group – Riddleland for kids

6) Please also mention what book you purchased.

7) Email us at Riddleland@riddlelandforkids.com

Other Fun Books By Riddleland
Riddles Series

Try Not to Laugh Challenge
Joke Series

Would You Rather Series

Get them on Amazon or our website at
www.riddlelandforkids.com

About Riddleland

Riddleland is a mum + dad run publishing company. We are passionate about creating fun and innovative books to help children develop their reading skills and fall in love with reading. If you have suggestions for us or want to work with us, shoot us an email at

riddleland@riddlelandforkids.com

Our family's favorite quote

"Creativity is an area in which younger people have a tremendous advantage since they have an endearing habit of always questioning past wisdom and authority."

– Bill Hewlett.

References

Ref :
Dk. (2014). Science a Children's Encyclopedia. DK Publishing.

Winston, R., & Burke, L. (2018). Science Squad. DK Children.

Made in the USA
Coppell, TX
08 September 2020